Baptism
New Life in Christ

by
Sr Eustochium Lee OSB

All booklets are published thanks to the generous support of the members of the Catholic Truth Society

CATHOLIC TRUTH SOCIETY
PUBLISHERS TO THE HOLY SEE

CONTENTS

1. WHAT AM I DOING HERE?

Dave is thinking: "Sleeping around, drinking a skinful every Friday night, and I've never robbed a bank but I didn't mind fiddling my timesheet at work if I could get away with it - but now that's all behind me. Tonight I am starting a new life." Beside him, Pete is thinking: "My life seems quite boring compared to Dave's. My wife and children are Catholics, I found myself being roped in to put up the Christmas crib and run the parish barbecue, and gradually I began to feel that this is a community which I want to be a real part of. I've done a lot of reading and thinking but I can't say I've had a big conversion experience." Meanwhile, next to Pete, Bernadette is holding her baby and thinking: "My faith is the most important thing in my life. I want my little girl to share it." On the other side of her is Sharon with her baby, thinking: "I've nothing against Jesus Christ, in fact he seems quite amazing; it's the Church which I can't stand, or at least I can't stand pushy Catholics like my mother-in-law in the row behind. But if I have the baby baptised he may have a better chance of getting into a Catholic school, and perhaps there are *some* nice things about being a Catholic."

Father Murphy goes on with his homily, but none of the candidates for baptism is listening. Dave is thinking: "I've told Fr Murphy he can pour on as much water as he likes. I don't care how wet I get. I want my whole previous life to be drowned dead in the water, so that I come out a new person." Pete is thinking: "What if my mouth goes dry when we have to answer the priest? Half of me wants to stand up in front of the parish and say that I believe in Jesus Christ, and half of me is terrified." Bernadette is thinking: "The bit I'm really looking forward to is after the baptism, when the baby is wrapped in a soft white shawl. It makes me think of the love that I want her to be surrounded by all her life, the love we give her and the knowledge that God is her loving Father and that Jesus is her friend." Sharon, meanwhile, is saying to herself: "All that stuff about being anointed with holy oil sounds like mumbo-jumbo to me. What do intelligent people like Dave and Pete really think about it? The bit where everyone holds lighted candles and one is brought to the baby is very pretty, but should I be holding one? After all, I'm not a goody-goody card-carrying Catholic, as my mother-in-law loves to point out. I wonder how long this sermon is going to last. Will my little boy blame me for committing him to a lifetime of boring sermons?"

These are four candidates for baptism at the Easter Vigil at an imaginary parish somewhere in England. What are they going to do and experience tonight? They or those who have brought them are thinking of new life, community, faith, relationship with Jesus Christ and with the Church. Baptism involves the use of ordinary things -

water, oil, white garments, lighted candles - which carry a special significance which sometimes seems obvious and sometimes takes a bit of unpacking; it also involves words, some of which are used in ordinary speech, like "believe," and some of which, like "baptism" and "sacrament," are religious jargon which needs to be defined. The purpose of this booklet is to provide a brief introduction to the service of baptism in the Roman Catholic Church, looking both at the practicalities of baptism and at its history and meaning.

2. Baptism in Jesus' World

Baptism before the coming of Jesus

From the beginnings of Christianity the way in to the Christian community was baptism. On the first Pentecost Sunday morning the crowd asked Peter, "What shall we do?" and he replied, "Repent and be baptised every one of you in the name of Jesus Christ for the forgiveness of your sins; and you shall receive the gift of the Holy Spirit" (*Acts* 3:38). To the modern mind, this may seem an odd response but the Jews and devout men who heard Peter would find it not unreasonable. The Jews were accustomed to the ideal of ritual washing which rendered the participant "clean" and fit for worship of God and the community life of the Chosen People; by the second century AD, and possibly as early as the time of Jesus, there was also the custom of baptism for pagan converts to Judaism. In the Greek and Roman pagan world too, taking a bath was much more of an event than today's quick shower necessary for hygiene: it was a social event, concluding with anointing with oil and putting on clean clothes. Both Jewish and pagan worlds, therefore, provided a vocabulary of actions and attitudes for the idea of baptising, but for the disciples of Jesus there was even more to it than this.

Jesus' baptism by John the Baptist

At the beginning of his public ministry, Jesus presented himself for baptism by John the Baptist in the River Jordan (*Mt* 3:13-17; *Mk* 1:9-11; *Lk* 3:21-22; *Jn* 1:31-34). John's baptism differed from both the Jewish ritual ablutions and from the baptising of pagan converts. The prophets of the Old Testament had insisted that ritual purity was not enough: there had to be a washing from sin too:

> Even though you make many prayers, I will not listen;
> your hands are full of blood.
> Wash yourselves; make yourselves clean;
> remove the evil of your doings from before my eyes
> (Is 1:15-16).

They looked to a cleansing which only God could perform:

> I will sprinkle clean water upon you,
> and you shall be clean from all your uncleannesses,
> and from all your idols I will cleanse you (Ezek 36:25).

In line with this desire for a fuller concept of purity, John's baptism was "a baptism of repentance for the forgiveness of sins" (*Mk* 1:4), and he offered it to Jews and pagans alike. The very location of the Jordan was significant. By preaching in the desert John was recalling the desert wanderings of the Israelites when they received the Law from God and were formed into the chosen people; when their wanderings were over, the Jordan was where they had crossed over into the Promised Land (*Josh* 4:19-24). At the basis of this national memory was the event of the Exodus from Egypt, when the Israelites fleeing slavery had escaped their overlords by a miraculous passage through the Red Sea (*Ex* 14:1-31). This was the defining moment in the history of the people of Israel. Subsequent promises of renewed favour by God would be given in terms of this escape:

> Fear not, for I have redeemed you;
> I have called you by name, you are mine.
> When you pass through the waters I will be with you;
> and through the rivers, they shall not overwhelm you
> (Is 43:1-2).

Even the rules of ritual purity were a reminder to Israel of her special status as the nation chosen to be God's servant, God's son:

> You are a people holy to the Lord your God; the Lord your God has chosen you to be a people for his own possession (Dt 7:6; see also Lv 11:44).

When Jesus had been baptised by John, "He saw the heavens opened and the Spirit descending on him like a dove; and a voice came from heaven, 'You are my beloved Son; with you I am well pleased'" (*Mk* 1:10-11). This acclamation recalls the prophecy of Isaiah,

> Behold my servant, whom I uphold,
> my chosen, in whom my soul delights;
> I have put my Spirit upon him (Is 42:1).

John the Baptist says of Jesus, "Behold, the Lamb of God, who takes away the sins of the world" (*Jn* 1:29), and this recalls Isaiah's concluding prophecy about this Servant:

> He poured out his soul to death,
> and was numbered with the transgressors;
> yet he bore the sin of many
> and made intercession for the transgressors (Is 53:12).

Jesus' baptism thus acts as a rehearsal for his whole life of total obedience to the Father's will, of fulfilling in his person all that God had asked of Israel and which Israel had failed to give. Subsequent Christian tradition saw Jesus' baptism by John as the beginning of his work of redemption, which reached its consummation on the Cross. As St Gregory Nazianzen wrote (in a sermon for the Epiphany in 381AD):

He comes to bury the whole of sinful humanity in the waters. He comes to sanctify the Jordan for our sake and in readiness for us; he who is spirit and flesh comes to begin a new creation through the Spirit and water.

Baptism in the earthly ministry of Jesus

After his baptism Jesus began to proclaim the coming of the kingdom of God, both by his preaching and by his actions, healing the sick, casting out demons and gathering a community of disciples whom he commanded to do the same and to live by his values and precepts. He was gracious to pagan outsiders (*Mk* 7:24-30; *Mt* 8:5-13), reached out to untouchable lepers (*Mk* 1:41) and forgave those whom the hardhearted condemned (*Lk* 7:50; 19:7; *Jn* 4:9; 8:11), showing that God's special choice of the

> *God's special choice of the people of Israel was not so much abolished as widened to include all men who believe in him.*

people of Israel was not so much abolished as widened to include all men who believe in him. Yet to follow Jesus is no easy option; it may involve leaving all that is dear (*Mk* 10:21); it may feel like voluntary crucifixion (*Mt* 16:24), but Christians believe there is salvation in no one else but Jesus Christ (*Ac* 4:12).

John the Baptist had spoken of One who was to come, who would baptise with the Holy Spirit (*Mt* 3:11; *Mk* 1:8; *Lk* 3:16; *Jn* 1:33). When Jesus speaks of baptism during his earthly ministry, however, he uses it as a metaphor for his approaching suffering and death: "Are you able to be baptised with the baptism with which I am baptised?" (*Mk* 10:38) and "I have a baptism to be baptised with, and how I am constrained until it is accomplished" (*Lk* 12:50). It by his death, his "going away", however, that the Spirit will come to his disciples (*Jn* 14:25-26; 16:7). The Gospels show him over and over again faced with the choice between courting popularity or losing it, between appeasing the religious and civil authorities and provoking them: always he chooses what is pleasing to the Father, and this culminates in his passion and death.

John's Gospel describes how, after the death of Jesus, a soldier opened his side with a spear "and at once there came out blood and water" (*Jn* 19:34). Details like this in John are never merely historical reportage. Anyone familiar with the Old Testament would think immediately of Ezekiel's vision of the future temple, from the side of which a fountain flowed whose waters brought life (*Ezek* 47:1-12). John quotes the prophet Zechariah, "They shall look upon him whom they have pierced" (*Jn* 19:37, cf *Zech* 12:10), but there is surely also an allusion to the later verse, "On that day there shall be a fountain opened for the house of David and the inhabitants of Jerusalem to cleanse them from sin and uncleanness" (*Zech* 13:1).

Baptism after the resurrection of Jesus

The Gospels preserve two sayings of the Risen Jesus concerning baptism: "Make disciples of all nations, baptising them in the name of the Father and of the Son and of the Holy Spirit" (*Mt* 28:19), and "He who believes and is baptised will be saved" (*Mk* 16:16). The first saying may be coloured by the liturgical practice known to the evangelist, just as references in the Acts of the Apostles to baptism "in the name of Jesus" may reflect an earlier usage of the Church; on the other hand, these may be less liturgical formulae than theological interpretation of the meaning of Christian baptism itself (see *Ac* 10:48; 19:5). The first formula expresses the belief that baptism enables us to enter into the relationship of Jesus with his Father and to share in it, through the power of the Holy Spirit; the second formula emphasises our identification with Jesus himself in baptism. What is without doubt is that the Church from earliest times baptised its converts. Later we shall look at how this is done. Here we shall consider why the Church should do this.

3. SACRAMENTS

Jesus, Sacrament of God

In many and various ways, God spoke of old to our fathers by the prophets; but in these last days he has spoken to us by a Son (Heb 1:1-2).

He is the image of the invisible God (Col 1:15).

Before baptism the candidate (or in the case of a baby, his parents and Godparents) makes a profession of faith: the first question asked is:

Do you believe in God, the Father almighty, creator of heaven and earth?

This belief is fundamental to the whole Christian faith; it is also fundamental to the whole system of sacramental rites of which baptism is the first. If there is a Creator of this world, there is something, someone, other than what we can see and touch, a dimension beyond what is attainable by the senses. Religion is the attempt to address that realm. If this world was created by God (as opposed to being created by a demon, or arising through some accident) then what is in it is good. The first reading at the Easter Vigil can be seen as a poem on this theme: "God created the heavens and the earth... and God saw that it was good" (*Gn* 1:1-2:4a). The Christian life may often involve the temporary or permanent renunciation of certain created things - by fasting, chastity, almsgiving, for example - but this is never because created things are in themselves bad. A Christian fasts not because food and the process of digestion are in some sense disgusting but in order to keep his mind alert for prayer, and perhaps so as to have something to give to the poor. He resists the temptation to have an affair with his secretary not because the act of sex is in itself bad but because the affair would demean the significance of sex in his exclusive union with his wife. The religious practice of Catholic Christians uses physical things - water, oil, bread, wine, and other things perceptible to the senses such as music or incense - in the confidence that they come from God and will help in making contact with God.

The second question the candidate or his parents is asked is:

> Do you believe in Jesus Christ, his only Son, our Lord, who was born of the Virgin Mary...?

The created world may be good but its limitations are clear. It is insufficient to satisfy the longings of man's heart for union with the Creator himself; creation is subject to death and decay; man himself inclines towards selfishness which, unchecked, causes misery to himself and to others. It is the Christian belief that Jesus Christ is God made man in order to deliver man from this threefold limitation of nature, death and sin. As St Leo told his congregation in Rome, on Christmas Day in 441AD:

> To you once cast aside, to you driven out from the thrones of Paradise, to you dying from long exiles, to you scattered into dust and ashes, who no longer had any hope of living - to you has power been given through the Incarnation of the Word. With it, you can return from far away to your Maker, can recognise your Father, can become free from slavery, can be made again a child rather than an outsider. With this power, you who were born of flesh that is subject to decay can be born again from the Spirit of God and can obtain through grace what you do not have through nature.

If God gave his Son in this way and for this purpose, Jesus in his earthly life, in his teachings, actions and most of all in his suffering and death was the best image, the best expression of God's attitude to mankind, the best indication of what God is like, and actually was God's presence for those who could see and touch him. He was, in fact, a visible sign of the invisible saving action of God, and by his visible presence and actions he both contained and furthered that saving action. The theological term (which will be discussed more fully later) for a visible sign of the invisible saving action of God, a sign which itself contains and furthers that saving action, is *sacrament,* and thus it can be said that Jesus of Nazareth is the pre-eminent sacrament of God.

The Church, Sacrament of Christ

The third and final question in the profession of faith is:

> Do you believe in the Holy Spirit, the holy Catholic Church, the communion of saints, the forgiveness of sins, the resurrection of the body, and life everlasting?

This may sound like an untidy list of extra doctrines, unconnected with each other, listed separately because they do not fit into the first question, about God the creator, or the second, about Jesus. It is in fact a question about our present situation and our future hope, and intimately connected with the other two.

Christians believe that Jesus rose from the dead and for some time could be seen and touched by the disciples but this period came to an end with his ascension. We are now in an interim phase, when Christ's work has been accomplished but we have yet to see its full effects. As St Gregory Nazianzen says, "The dispensations of the Body of Christ are ended... and that of the Spirit is beginning" (sermon given for Pentecost, probably in 381AD). Human beings are present to each other by their bodies, so during the earthly life of Jesus his visible body was his way of being present to the people around him. We believe that his body is risen and in glory, but our present experience of it is a kind of absence. What we see and experience is the presence of each other.

There were two ways Jesus promised to be with his followers after his death and resurrection: in the poor and oppressed ("As you did it to one of the least of these my brethren, you did it to me": *Mt* 25:40) and in the believing community of his disciples, that is, the Church. In the believing community he is most truly present when they fulfil his commands, praying (*Mt* 18:20), pondering his words (*Jn* 14:23), receiving and handing on his teaching (*Mt* 28:20), and most of all when they celebrate the Eucharist (*Mt* 26:26-28; *Mk* 14:22-24; *Lk* 22:19-20; see also *Jn* 6:52-58 and *1 Cor* 11:26).

The Church itself is "a visible sign of the invisible saving action of God, a sign which itself contains and furthers that saving action" and can therefore be called a sacrament. It may sometimes appear a rather poor sign, but we view it with the eyes of faith that believe it is quickened by the Spirit whom Jesus promised to send, invisibly uniting all holy people who have ever lived, and pleading for and obtaining from God forgiveness for the less holy, including those currently contributing to the poverty of the sign. At the baptismal ceremony (and everywhere else) we have before our physical eyes only our limited and mortal human bodies; it is our hope not that we shall be delivered from these but that they will be transformed in ways beyond all imagining, so that the limitations of nature, death and sin are taken away. It is because of this hope that the Church has rites called sacraments or mysteries, whereby our limited and mortal bodies make contact with the risen body of Christ. If we had lived in Palestine in the time of Jesus our mortal bodies would have been present to his mortal body; when the kingdom of God comes in all its fullness our transformed bodies will be present to his risen body. In the time of the Church, that is, the period between Jesus' resurrection and our own, the sacraments of the Church make our mortal bodies present to his risen body, make his power present to and efficacious for us. As St Leo says:

> He made an end to his bodily presence in the sight of his disciples on the fortieth day after the resurrection. He was to remain at the Father's right hand until the time predetermined by God for fulfilling the number of the children of the Church should come, and he would return to judge the living and the dead in the same flesh with which he ascended. What was to be seen of our Redeemer has passed over into the sacraments of the Church (Sermon for the feast of the Ascension, 445AD).

The seven sacraments of the Church

Sometimes Catholics speak of "the seven sacraments" as if they were seven different recipes for obtaining God's grace, as one may list apple pie, apple crumble, apple turnover and so on. It may be better to think first of the Eucharist as the sacrament par excellence of Christ's presence; Baptism and Confirmation as the initiation of members into the community which celebrates the Eucharist; Anointing of the Sick and Penance (Confession) as the means of restoring to that community members weakened through illness or estranged by sin; Holy Orders (ordination) as the means of forming and nourishing the community, by preaching the Gospel and celebrating the Eucharist; Marriage as the pre-eminent sign of the faithful union between Christ and the Church, bringing forth new life.

The sacraments involve a visible element which anyone can see - for example, water being poured, bread being shared - and an invisible element, the share in God's own life, which can be perceived only with the eyes of faith. The Scholastic theologians of the Middle Ages tried to analyse them in terms taken from the philosophy of Aristotle and therefore identified in each sacrament its "matter" (a symbolic gesture or thing) and its "form" (words which bring out its significance, make explicit what is already there). In the case of baptism its *matter* is the pouring of water over a person and its *form* is the words "I baptise you in the name of the Father and of the Son and of the Holy Spirit."

Another way of reflecting on the sacraments is to consider them in terms of three levels of reality as follows:

the *visible rite,* which symbolises and brings about
the *sacramental reality* which is known by faith and which in a person of good disposition brings about
the *final reality* - "final" in the sense of what it is ultimately aimed at.

In the case of baptism, we could say that the *visible rite* is the pouring of water with the formula mentioned above, the *sacramental reality* is the incorporation into the Church and the *final reality* is rebirth to divine life through the Spirit of love.

4. WHAT DIFFERENCE DOES BAPTISM MAKE?

Baptism introduces the new Christian into a whole new order of being, in which past, present and future are joined together. All the sacraments can be said to look back to the earthly life of Jesus (and to the history of Israel which led up to him), to have an effect in the present and to look forward to, and even hasten, the completion of God's plan in the coming of the Lord Jesus at the end of time. Baptism initiates a person into this process, opening up for him a whole new way of being human and offering him a destiny beyond anything that he could achieve on his own.

Jesus's Baptism forshadowed in Old Testament

Christian baptism, of course, links the person being baptised with Jesus' own baptism by John. Ephraim the Syrian has a long poem beginning:

> The Spirit descended from the heights
>   and sanctified the water as it hovered.
> When John baptised Jesus
>   it left all and settled on one,
> but now it has come down and settled
>   upon all who are reborn in baptism.

The other and even greater "baptism" in Jesus' life is the baptism of his suffering, death and rising from the dead, and Christian baptism is a participation in this. St Paul tells the Romans:

> All of us who were baptised into Christ Jesus were baptised into his death. We were buried with him in baptism into death, so that as Christ was raised from the dead by the glory of the Father, we too might walk in newness of life (*Rom* 6:3-4).

Christian tradition also identified events and ideas in the Old Testament as "types" or pointers towards baptism. First and foremost of these was the Exodus from Egypt and the passage through the Red Sea. In a homily on the Baptism of Christ, probably preached on the feast of the Epiphany 383AD, St Gregory of Nyssa wrote:

> The people itself, by passing through the Red Sea, proclaimed the good tidings of salvation by water. The people passed over, and the Egyptian king with his host was engulfed, and by these actions this sacrament

All of us who were baptised into Christ Jesus were baptised into his death. We were buried with him in baptism into death, so that as Christ was raised from the dead by the glory of the Father, we too might walk in newness of life (Rom 6:3-4).

was foretold. For even now, whensoever the people is in the water of regeneration, fleeing from Egypt, from the burden of sin, it is set free and saved. But the devil with his own servants (I mean, of course, the spirits of evil) is choked with grief, and perishes, deeming the salvation of men to be his own misfortune.

Another great "type" of baptism is the creation of the world. At the Easter Vigil we hear the creation story where "the earth was without form and void, and darkness was upon the face of the deep, and the Spirit of God was moving over the face of the waters" (*Gn* 1:2). God's effortless work of creation, when his Spirit seemed to fertilise the formless waters, so that they brought forth living creatures, is from this point of view a foreshadowing of the re-creation of Christians in the waters of the font. In his sermons *On the Sacraments,* around AD 370, St Ambrose comments on this passage:

> For you it was reserved that water should bring you forth to grace, as that other water brought forth creatures to natural life.

Other "types" of baptism are the Flood, in which those with Noah in the ark are saved (*Gn* 6:5-9:17; cf *1 Pt* 3:18-22), Moses' being saved as a baby in a basket in the bulrushes (*Ex* 1:15-2:10), the Israelites' passage over the Jordan into the Promised Land (*Jos* 3:7-4:24), Naaman being cured of leprosy in the Jordan (*2 Kg* 5:1-19).

Effects of baptism: Salvation

The rite of baptism is not just the individual's profession of faith, or a ceremony symbolising his reception into the Christian community. It makes an objective difference to the person receiving it. In a sermon probably preached in the second half of the fourth century AD, St Cyril of Jerusalem, speaking to the newly baptised, says:

> *If a person has been baptised, even if he afterwards lives a life unworthy of his baptism, the baptism is not undone.*

What a strange and astonishing situation! We did not really die, we were not really buried, we did not really hang from a cross and rise again. *Our imitation was symbolic, but our salvation a reality.* Christ truly hung from a Cross, was buried, and truly rose again. All this he did gratuitously for us, so that we might share his sufferings by imitating them, and gain salvation in actuality.

If a person has been baptised, even if he afterwards lives a life unworthy of his baptism, the baptism is not undone. A person baptised as a baby, who grew up ignorant of the faith and who then discovered Christ as an adult, could not be re-baptised. He would instead undergo a suitable period of instruction and formation in the Christian life, with a view to receiving the other Sacraments of Initiation (Confirmation and Holy Communion) and becoming a full member of the Christian community. As St Paul says regarding the Israelites, the Chosen People who did not accept Christ, "The gifts and call of God are irrevocable" (*Rom* 11:29). As long as baptism was carried out properly, and the person receiving it did not inwardly deny the faith he was outwardly professing, the baptism was real and all its power is, as it were, there for the taking. This "objective difference" made by baptism is called by theologians a *character;* it is like the inscription on a coin which may be obscured by dirt but which can never be removed.

Linked with the term "character" is the *seal* (in Greek, *sphragis;* in Latin, *signaculum*). It is used of God the Son in the Letter to the Hebrews: "He reflects the glory of God and bears the very stamp [*sphragis*] of his nature" (*Heb* 1:3) and St Paul applies it to Christians: "God has put his seal upon us" (*2 Cor* 1:22). It was originally used for the mark of ownership branded on animals or the tattoo on an enlisted soldier, for the seal on legal documents or the imprint on coins. A baptised person is no longer his own property; he belongs to God. Theodore of Mopsuestia, preaching to his converts around 420 AD, told them: "You carry the identification mark of a soldier of Christ our Lord."

Effects of baptism: Forgiveness of sins

By baptism all the sins of one's past life are forgiven by God. They are like Pharaoh's armies who were drowned in the Red Sea while the Israelites escaped: "Not so much as one of them remained" (*Ex* 14:28). Referring to her baptism, the Sudanese ex-slave Blessed Josephine Bakhita (1869-1947) used to say: "The Lord must judge me only from my eighteenth birthday onward. Before that, there is nothing to judge, because God has wiped away all my sins." St Augustine, in his treatise *On Baptism* (c. 400 AD), even discusses the extreme example of someone who presented himself for baptism without truly repenting of his past sins, comparing him to the unjust steward in the parable who, forgiven by his master, nonetheless refused to forgive the debts of his fellow-servant (see *Mt* 18:23-35):

> Yet the fact that he had not yet forgiven his fellow-servant did not prevent his lord from forgiving him all his debts... So the grace of baptism is not prevented from giving remission of all sins, even if he to whom they are forgiven continues to cherish hatred towards his brother in his heart. For the guilt of yesterday is remitted, and all that was before it, nay, even the guilt of the very hour and moment previous to baptism, and during baptism itself.

If this unhappy person continues in his sinful hatred after baptism, but then at a later stage repents, he is not re-baptised; rather, the graces of baptism, which his hatred had blocked, are now able to flow freely. St Augustine continues:

> What was given before [in baptism] becomes then powerful to work his salvation, when the former deceit is done away by the truthful confession.

If the sins forgiven by God in baptism included actions for which justice demanded that amends be made or at least attempted (for example, returning what one had stolen, trying to restore someone's good name which one had damaged), the responsibility to do this would of course remain after baptism. It is to be hoped that the new life which begins at baptism would render the sinner more sensitive to the harm he had done in the past, more resourceful about how to put it right with the injured party, more alert to avoiding such hurtful actions in the future.

Effects of baptism: Freedom from original sin

We tend to confine the terms sin, guilt and forgiveness to deliberate sinful acts, but there is also the whole area of human nature which through heredity, bad experience, frailty, fear or panic has responses less than the best. This flaw in human nature is what is know as "original sin"; it separates us from God even when there has been no personal, deliberate sin. Jesus Christ did not have this flaw.

The only other human being who did not have this flaw was the virgin Mary, but this does not make her any less redeemed than other Christians; rather, it is by Christ's action that she had from the first moment of her existence the complete freedom from sin which will be ours only in the world to come. For his part, God the Son accepted his situation of separation from God (both by becoming a finite creature, and by experiencing the loss of God's felt presence) as an act of sacrificial love. By raising him from the dead, God made him the first fruits of the new creation, the beginning of the new order which is his plan for the entire human race. We are to make the same passage from death to eternal life as he did. The liturgy of baptism speaks not of "washing away the guilt of original sin" but of being set free from original sin, being brought out of the power of darkness (see the Prayers for Exorcism in the *Rite of Baptism for Children*). What happened literally in the death of Christ, happens sacramentally to his disciples. "You were buried with him in baptism, in which you were also raised with him through faith in the working of God, who raised him from the dead. You, who were dead in

Original Sin: Following the fall from grace of our first parents when they chose to go their own way rather than God s, they passed to their descendants a wounded human nature, susceptible to sin. The state is called original sin . (The Faith of the Catholic Church, CTS).

trespasses... God made alive together with him, having forgiven us all our trespasses" (*Col* 2:12-13).

Effects of baptism: Rescue from power of the devil

Not only are human beings flawed, they live in a flawed world. Other ages or societies, including the world in which the New Testament was written, were more at ease with the concept of devils, invisible intelligent beings who pitted themselves against men's efforts for good. No doubt some phenomena, such as mental illness, were once ascribed to demonic activity, which today's scientific knowledge analyses differently and probably more accurately. Nevertheless there remains a realm which does not seem to fit into the category of neurological malfunctioning or even human sins. Prior to baptism, for both adults and babies, there are prayers of exorcism which ask God's protection against the powers of this realm. This is not to deny the free will or goodness of the candidate, but simply to acknowledge that he is operating in a spiritually polluted environment.

Effects of baptism: Gift of the Holy Spirit

Any good person is unwittingly acting according to the promptings of the Holy Spirit, but by baptism the Christian becomes a temple where the Holy Spirit dwells (cf *1 Cor* 6:19). Preaching during Lent 390 AD, St John Chrysostom told the candidates for baptism:

By the words of the bishop and by his hand the presence of the Holy Spirit flies down upon you and another man comes up out of the font.

Effects of baptism: Membership of the Church

Before baptism an adult convert may have often gone to Mass with his Catholic friends; an unbaptised baby may have been taken by his parents. Unbaptised, however, he was present as an outsider, at best a welcome guest. After baptism he truly belongs. He is part of the "royal priesthood" (*1 Pet* 2:9) whose job it is to declare God's wonderful deeds and to offer the sacrifice of praise. St Edith Stein (1891-1942), a philosopher whose faith journey was from Judaism, through atheism, to baptism as an adult, explained this in an essay on the Prayer of the Church:

> In baptism and the sacrament of reconciliation, Christ's blood cleanses us of our sins, opens our eyes to eternal light, our ears to hearing God's word. It opens our lips to sing his praise, to pray in expiation, in petition, in thanksgiving, all of which are but varying forms of adoration, ie, of the creature's homage to the Almighty and All-benevolent One.

As a member of the Church, the baptised person puts into practice the faith he professes, aiming to be a living copy of the Gospels for all who have not seen them. One recent example of someone who lived this to the full was

Archbishop Oscar Romero, champion of the poor in El Salvador. A few months before he was assassinated while saying Mass on 24 March 1980, he said in a sermon:

> If they kill all the priests and the bishop too... everyone of you must be a messenger, a prophet; the Church will always exist in the world for as long as there remains one baptised person; and that last baptised person who remains in the world, it is he who has before the entire world the responsibility to maintain the flag of our Lord's truth and divine justice flying high.

in baptism renewal is brought about in one moment by the remission of all sins

The future life of the baptised person

The whole Christian life is a dying and rising with Christ; baptism is the essential transition from the old life to the new; but we live in between Christ's resurrection and our own, and have our span of life in order to bring to fruition the seed planted at baptism. The barrier between man and God caused by original sin has been taken away, but the effects of original sin remain. Thirty years after his own baptism (as an adult) at the Easter Vigil in 387 AD St Augustine wrote:

> This renewal, of course, is not brought about in the one moment of conversion itself, as in baptism that renewal

is brought about in one moment by the remission of all sins (for there does not remain even one sin, however small it may be, that is not forgiven). But just as it is one thing to be free from fevers, and another thing to recover from the weakness which has resulted from the fevers, so the first step in a cure is to remove the cause of the disease, which is done through the remission of all sins; the second is to heal the disease itself, which is done gradually.

The lifetime of struggle against the effects of original sin, as one draws upon the grace given in baptism, learning to live not as fearful slaves but as sons and heirs in God's house, is in fact our share in the expansion of the kingdom which Christ proclaimed and which on the last day will be made manifest. The graces of baptism include first of all membership of the Church, with all its privileges and supports, such as participation in the Eucharist and receiving the Body and Blood of the Lord; sharing in the Church's liturgical life; the life of personal prayer and study of the Scriptures; the counsel of pastors and wise Christian friends; the example of other Catholics; the intercession and example of Our Lady and all the saints.

There was a period in the early Church when it was thought that there could be no forgiveness for serious sin after baptism (murder, adultery, for example); gradually it came to be understood that the Church had the power and authority to forgive these and lesser sins; and the

Sacrament of Penance (Confession) is the means of bringing the repentant sinner back to how he stood before God on the day of his baptism. One modern convert writes:

> When I renounced Satan during the ritual of the baptismal promises, I felt a distinct weight fall from my soul. The sacrament washed me clean, and "created a pure heart within me"; but whatever became of my heart after that was clearly my own responsibility. I did not become incapable of sin, just capable of not sinning. Like all converts, I soon found that was not protection enough. But there stands the sacrament of penance, precisely to restore in us the innocence of baptism.[1]

The goal of it all is union with God in love. St Augustine concluded:

> If the last day of this life shall find anyone in such progress and growth holding fast to the faith of the Mediator, he will be received by the holy angels in order that he may be brought to the God whom he has worshiped, and by whom he is to be brought to perfection; and at the end of the world he shall receive an incorruptible body, not for punishment but for glory.

---

[1] Stratford Caldecott, "Gnosis and Grace," in *The Path to Rome: modern journeys to the Catholic Church,* edited by Dwight Longenecker (Gracewing, 1999), p178.

5. The Participants in Baptism: The Candidate

Adult candidates for baptism

An adult who asks to be baptised is usually at the end of long period of discernment. Origen, writing in the third century, says:

> When a man has been touched to the heart by the divine word, when the word is no longer, as it were like a perfume which he breathes, or even an intoxicating wine which he drinks, but rather like the living blood which will enable him to bleed to death on the cross - then he is ready for Christian initiation.

There are as many journeys to faith as there are people on the earth; some converts have a great sense of personal encounter with Christ, others have simply decided on the truth of the Christian faith after careful study. Neither form of conversion is superior to the other; rather, all who wish to be Catholics should aim at a truly "catholic" approach, ready to be led by whatever means the Lord proposes. The faith necessary for baptism is not a warm glow but a personal adherence to God, and a free assent to all that God has revealed. It is more a matter of the will and the intellect rather than the emotions.

Before his baptism in Nigeria at the age of nine, Blessed Cyprian Tansi (1903-1964) tore up his personal juju (pagan fetish), thus showing his renouncement of pagan worship and belief in false gods. For converts in Britain the false gods may be superstitions like horoscopes or tarot cards, or the modern idols of money or prestige, or sexual pleasure separated from genuine love. Baptism demands a definitive break with these. In addition, a person could not be accepted for baptism if his way of life was fundamentally opposed to the precepts of the Gospel - if, for example, he earned his living through the unjust exploitation of others, or was carrying on an extra-marital affair. More complicated is the situation where someone is living faithfully in a relationship which cannot be blessed by the Church - for example, where either one of the partners has a former spouse still living. If someone desires baptism but fears that he would be prevented from receiving it for a reason such as this, he should seek the advice of the Church (it could be that, upon examination, the earlier marriage is found not to be valid, and so is no obstacle to baptism).

Baptism demands a definitive break with false gods

The sincerity of a person's faith would be shown by the fact that even before baptism he was already trying to pray and to live as a Christian. He would, of course, be subject to the same weaknesses and temptations as anyone else, and should certainly not wait to become perfect before seeking baptism. It is baptism, and all that goes with it and flows from it, which will arm him for the struggle. The Church would recognise that there is a difference between battling with a weakness, even if it involves repeated falls and new beginnings, and the refusal to see any need for change in the way one behaves.

Most adults are baptised after a period of instruction, given either privately or in a parish's group of "enquirers". This period, known as the Rite of Christian Initiation of Adults (RCIA), climaxes in the baptism of the adult converts but before that there is a long journey of discovery about the faith and gradual initiation into the Christian community, each stage of which is marked by a special service. The stages are:

> *Precatechumenate,* when a person is simply enquiring and receiving basic instruction in the faith;
>
> *Catechumenate,* when a person has expressed a serious intention to be baptised; it begins with the *Rite of Becoming Catechumens* (catechumen means one who is being taught) and is followed by more intensive prayer and instruction, which may last months or even years;
>
> *Rite of Election,* which usually takes place at the beginning of Lent; at this rite the catechumen is formally enrolled for baptism at Easter;

The Scrutinies, special prayers for the candidates for baptism, said at Mass on the Sundays of Lent;

The Presentations, at which the candidates are formally presented with the Profession of Faith (commonly called the Creed , a statement of basic beliefs which all Catholics know by heart) and the prayer taught by Jesus, the Our Father ;

The Preparatory Rites, usually on Holy Saturday morning, when the candidates publicly recite the Creed, choose a Christian name, are anointed with the oil of catechumens and receive final exhortations and blessings;

The Celebration of the Sacraments of Initiation, usually during the Easter Vigil; the candidates are baptised and confirmed, and receive Holy Communion for the first time.

Postbaptismal Catechesis, or *Mystagogia,* during which the newly baptised are helped to settle into their new life, both by the prayer and fraternal welcome of the Christian community and by any further instruction which they need.

A person who was seriously ill and in danger of death, if he expressed a sincere desire for baptism, could of course be baptised without delay. He would be asked to promise, if he recovered, to undergo the usual instruction in the faith and receive Confirmation and Holy Communion in due course.

The season of Lent probably developed from the final period of instruction for catechumens who were to be baptised at Easter; it is an opportunity for baptised

Christians to re-live the catechumenate prior to their renewal of baptismal vows at the Easter Vigil.

Child candidates for baptism

If the candidate for baptism is a child who has reached the age of reason (usually seven years or more) there is a special version of the *Rite of Christian Initiation of Adults* called the *Rite of Initiation for Children of Catechetical Age*. The child would receive instruction adapted to his needs, and be admitted to this Rite only when he showed sufficient faith and understanding, albeit not of an adult nature. The wording of the various rites is simpler and more flexible, so that the child can give his own conscientious response of faith. This case usually arises when a child's parents are converted to the faith, or return to the Church after years away during which they did not have their children baptised. If the child of non-Catholic parents asked to be baptised, he would have to have his parents' consent, and the Church would want to be sure that he would have sufficient support from Godparents and others so that he could be expected to become a fully mature Christian as he grew up.

The baptism of babies (infant baptism)

Where one or both parents is a believer, the Church gladly baptises babies. There is a special rite for them called the *Rite of Baptism for Children* - that is, for children not old enough to speak for themselves. The rite confirms that the fullness of baptismal grace is given to the baby, and yet also recognises that it will be years before he can respond fully to this grace and make the same profession of faith which an adult convert makes. Ideally, a loving upbringing in a home where Christ is known, loved and worshiped, together with suitable instruction in the Catholic faith, will correspond to the catechumenate which an adult convert undergoes. A baptised baby is like the infant heir to an enormous fortune: the wealth truly belongs to him, but he needs education and maturity to be able to enjoy it and use it well.

> *A baptised baby is like the infant heir to an enormous fortune: the wealth truly belongs to him, but he needs education and maturity to be able to enjoy it and use it well.*

Throughout the centuries there have been people inside and outside the Church who have said that babies should not be baptised. These assertions usually arise from disagreement about the nature of baptism itself. If baptism was merely a ceremony marking the baptised person's own public profession of faith, there would be no point in baptising babies who could not be claimed to have this faith.

The baptism of the babies of Christian families, however, is the result of certain doctrines:

- that there is an inherent flaw in human nature which separates us from God;
- that the initiative in the whole history of salvation, from creation onwards, is always God s;
- that God offers a share in his life to all men but forces no one to accept it;
- that the Church is not just a group of like-minded people, a sort of Jesus Christ Appreciation Society, but the body of Christ in the world;

The flaw which separates us from God

Some ask whether it is fair to baptise a baby, rather than to let him make up his own mind later on. This question implies that the unbaptised baby is in a neutral state, and to baptise him is like enrolling him for a career as a paratrooper regardless of whether he may grow up to be a sensitive type who really wants to be an artist. The Catholic response is that the baby is not in a neutral state: he has been born into a world which God made and loves but which does not know God, a world which did not recognise Jesus Christ when he came to it. Above and beyond defects of upbringing and environment there is a skewedness in man which prompts him to selfishness and greed. The baby had no personal choice about being born into this world, born with this condition. Baptism is the first step in curing this skewed condition, in setting the baby free from this world of unbelief. The baby is then in the position of an adult baptised in an emergency before he has been properly instructed in the faith. The grace of baptism is there; it will be for the baby, as he grows to adulthood, to lay hold of this grace and let his life be utterly different from what it *Before I formed you in the womb I knew you* would have been if he had not been baptised. If fairness is the issue, it could equally be asked if it is fair *not* to baptise the baby, and thus to deprive him of the grace of baptism.

God always takes the first initiative

"Let him discover Christ for himself and choose to be baptised if he wants." The problem with this approach is that it implies that man makes the first move. The Christian belief is "God created the heavens and the earth... God so loved the world... Before I formed you in the womb I knew you... God shows his love for us in that while we were yet sinners Christ died for us" (*Gn* 1:1; *Jn* 3:16; *Jer* 1:5; *Rom* 5:8). Always God acts first and man responds. This is in contrast with all the pagan religions which were such a snare for the people of Israel in the Old Testament, where the attitude was that if *you* made the requisite sacrifices the god would automatically be on your side. The God of Israel says:

> When Israel was a child, I loved him,
>   and out of Egypt I called my son (*Hos* 11:1).

This is God the loving Father of whom Jesus says, "Your Father knows what you need before you ask him" (*Mt* 6:8), who Paul says created all nations, "that they should seek God, in the hope that they might feel after him and find him" (*Ac* 17:27). The baptism of babies is an affirmation that of ourselves we are helpless, that God's loving-kindness goes before us and even our turning towards him is at his prompting. A person who was baptised as a baby should not waste energy feeling regretful that he has not had the experience of adult baptism. Rather, he should make his own Moses' words to the Israelites as they approached the Promised Land: "You have seen how the Lord your God bore you, as a man carries his son, in all the way that you went, until you came to this place" (*Dt* 1:31).

God offers a share in his life to all

The sacraments are not magical spells but God's way of communicating his life to human beings, through human

When Israel was a child, I loved him,
and out of Egypt I called my son (Hos 11:1).

words and gestures. This gift is not dependent on the holiness or maturity or any other quality of the human recipient (the person being baptised) or indeed of the human agent (the person doing the baptising). As long as the person being baptised does not deny the faith professed in the baptismal ceremony, God's life is indeed communicated.

As St Augustine writes in his commentary on John's Gospel:

> This word of faith has so much power in the Church of God that, through the very one who believes, offers, blesses, immerses, it cleanses even the tiny infant, not yet having the capacity with its heart to believe to justice and with its mouth to make a profession of faith to salvation. All this is done through the word, of which the Lord says, "Now you are clean by reason of the word that I have spoken to you" (*Jn* 15:3).

The theological term for this feature of sacraments is *ex opere operato* which means literally "by the work worked", that is, its efficacy depends on God's power working through the action itself, not the people involved. A sacrament thus differs from another pious activity such as making the sign of the cross, which is said to be *ex opere operantis,* "by the work of the person working"; it may help someone grow in holiness but its ability to do this depends on the devotion with which the person does it. A baby, who obviously is not actively denying the faith, therefore receives in baptism all the grace which an adult candidate does. As the baby grows up he will develop his free will and powers of judgment. The Church hopes and prays he will use these to make a conscientious choice in favour of Jesus Christ. If he does not do so, nothing can force him. He is like a prodigal son who left home so young that he cannot remember it: if he does discover the way back, all his rights of inheritance will be there waiting for him, and his family the Church will receive him with joy.

The Church is the body of Christ in the world

"My Catholic in-laws drive me mad but I still want to have my baby baptised." To ask to have one's baby baptised is in itself an acknowledgment that the Church is greater than one's present experience of it. The bond of baptism unites the child with Christians everywhere in the world and indeed with all the saints and heroes of the faith down the ages; more importantly even than this, the newly baptised baby is, unawares, part of the group of whom Jesus spoke at the Last Supper: "I do not pray for these only, but also for those who believe in me through their word" (*Jn*

I do not pray for these only, but also for those who believe in me through their word (Jn 17:20).

17:20). St Paul told the Corinthians who were tempted to boast of their spiritual riches that God chose what is foolish, weak, low, despised in the eyes of the world (cf *1 Cor* 1:26-29). To be an authentic sign, a sign which actually wrought the redemption of the human race, a sacrament of God's love, Jesus let himself be arrested, falsely condemned, mocked, scourged and crucified. A helpless baby, who could not appear to be bringing some great qualities into the Church as a talented adult convert might, is thus one reminder of this aspect of the body of Christ of which baptism makes him a member.

Baptism of Desire

"What about my baby who died before he was baptised? And my friend who has never been baptised?" Jesus told Nicodemus, "Unless one is born of water and the Spirit, he cannot enter the kingdom of God" (*Jn* 3:5). Nevertheless, the Church says of the unbaptised:

> Those who through no fault of their own do not know the Gospel of Christ or his Church, but who nevertheless seek God with a sincere heart, and, moved by grace, try in their actions to do his will as they know it through the dictates of their conscience - these too may attain eternal salvation (Vatican II, Dogmatic Constitution on the Church, *Lumen Gentium*).

This does not deny the words of Jesus on the necessity of baptism or indeed the necessity of faith in him but simply acknowledges God's freedom to draw men to himself by whatever means he chooses to use. In the early Church when martyrdom was a real possibility, the Church always held that someone martyred for faith in Christ before he had had a chance to be baptised had received "baptism by blood" and would undoubtedly receive all the benefits of water baptism. The logical extension of this view is that a catechumen who died before he had been baptised had received "baptism of desire" and he too could be considered a baptised person. Then there are the "good pagans" who if they had heard the Gospel would undoubtedly have accepted it; and to them must be added the non-believers who have heard about the Gospel but have not had it presented to them in a convincing or compelling way. When they come before God for judgment, and all is made plain to them that before was obscure, they will surely want everything that, for believers, baptism represents; and God who is rich in mercy and desires the salvation of all is surely free to grant what they desire. Christians are certainly obliged in charity to seek to share the joys of the life of faith in Christ, but at the same time they can look on their non-believing friends as having baptism by desire, even if the friends would themselves not recognise the term (See *The Catechism of the Catholic Church*, §1257-

1261). We know who are visibly members of the Church, and as to the rest we are simply unable to tell, for they lie outside the sacramental sphere and it is only the sacraments which make the Spirit visible to us.

Difficult issues: Babies who die before baptism

If a baby has been baptised and then dies, his parents can be absolutely confident that their little one is enjoying the fullness of union with God and even interceding for them, and will one day join God in welcoming them into heaven. The fate of babies who die unbaptised, however, together with that of babies who are miscarried and those killed by abortion, often causes anguish to their parents and others concerned for them. There is no straightforward answer in Scripture or the Church's tradition. The simple theory goes like this: baptism is necessary for salvation; it may be possible for an unbaptised adult who dies to have baptism of desire; this cannot be assumed of those below the age of reason; therefore unbaptised babies cannot go to heaven. St Augustine assumed, reluctantly, that unbaptised babies went to hell, though not such a severe hell as that reserved for hardened sinners since the babies were "guilty" of original sin only. Some have posited that there was a special place for unbaptised babies called Limbo where the babies would enjoy natural happiness but not the supernatural happiness of the vision of God.

Limbo is a theory; it is not the official teaching of the Catholic Church.[2] Even Limbo is of little comfort to grieving parents who would like to think that one day they shall be reunited with these little ones whom they had for so short a time. We should recall that in the Old Testament it is the image of the constant love of a mother who can never forget the child of her womb which Isaiah uses to express God's faithful love for sinful Israel (cf *Is* 49:15); and it was of unbaptised Jewish children that Jesus said, "See that you do not despise one of these little ones; for I tell you that in heaven their angels always behold the face of my Father" (*Mt* 18:10). *The Catechism of the Catholic Church* states:

> The great mercy of God who desires that all men should be saved, and Jesus' tenderness toward children... allow us to hope that there is a way of salvation for the children who die without baptism (§1261).

Those who mourn the death of an unbaptised child, especially a miscarried or aborted child, may wish to meditate on the Scripture readings proposed for the funeral of unbaptised children (*Isaiah* 25:6a, 7-8a; *Lamentations* 3:17-26; *Mark* 15:33-46), and ask God to renew their faith in his infinite mercy and power.

---

[2] The only mention of Limbo in official Church documents is in a letter of Pope Pius VI of 1794 condemning the heresies of the Jansenists. One of the Jansenist assertions was that Limbo was a heretical opinion, and that hell was the only fate for unbaptised babies. The Pope condemned this view, without giving a ruling on Limbo as such.

Difficult issues: Baptising a baby in secret

"My daughter-in-law hasn't had the grandchildren baptised. Why don't I do it secretly next time I am baby-sitting?" Although this course of action may seem attractive to an anxious Catholic grandparent, it is not approved of by the Church. Baptism is offered to the children of believing parents (or at least one believing parent), where there are good indications that the seed of faith which baptism implants in the child will be brought to full maturity as the child grows up. *to fulfil the true meaning of the sacrament, children must later be formed in the faith in which they have been baptised* The Church would not seek to baptise the children of non-believers, even if they were admirable people in other ways. By analogy, the Church is convinced of the Real Presence of our Lord in the Blessed Sacrament, irrespective of the faith or lack of it of the recipient; yet the Church does not give Holy Communion to those who have no faith or who have not been properly instructed; similarly, the Church does not doubt God's power working in the sacrament of baptism; but, as the introduction to the rite of baptism states, "to fulfil the true meaning of the sacrament, children must later be formed in the faith in which they have been baptised." In the past, when the extended family were expected to play a greater role in the care of children, and moreover when Christian values could be taken for granted in society, the personal commitment of the baby's parents seemed perhaps less important. Today, however, it is essential that at least one of the parents should himself seek the baptism of the child and be ready to promise to train him in the practice of the faith. Furthermore, the refusal to have children baptised may be in fact a cloak for some other subconscious agenda, such as wanting to show independence of the family's opinions. Catholic grandparents would be wise to avoid letting baptism become a bone of contention. They should aim rather to show the beauty of the faith by their kindness and goodness. They should always be ready to give a thoughtful, reasoned account of the faith if asked, but otherwise should support the potential faith of the grandchildren and their parents chiefly by prayer and example.

6. THE PARTICIPANTS IN BAPTISM: THE MINISTER AND THE CHRISTIAN COMMUNITY

The minister: bishops, priests, deacons and lay-people

Most people are baptised by the parish priest, or by another priest or deacon, but it is particularly fitting when the baptism is carried out by the bishop of the diocese. It is easy to view the Church as an international organisation with its headquarters in Rome and local branches in other places, but in fact each diocese is "the Church" in that place, in all its fullness, with the faithful gathered around their bishop, successor to the apostles. Guarantee of purity of doctrine is signified by the fact that the bishop of the diocese is in communion with the Bishop of Rome and all the other Churches which are in communion with him. In the same baptismal homily already cited, Theodore of Mopsuestia explained:

> When you have pronounced these vows and this covenant, the bishop comes over to you. Instead of his usual clothes, he is wearing a delicate, shining vestment. He is wearing new garments which denote the new world you are entering; their dazzling appearance signifies that you will shine in the next life; its light texture symbolises the delicacy and grace of that world.

The bishop could not possibly preside at all baptisms in his diocese, but it is right to see the parish priest or deacon as the bishop's representative. The chrism (perfumed oil) with which a baby is anointed after baptism comes from the supply which has been consecrated by the bishop at the "Chrism Mass" at the cathedral during Holy Week, when the priests and representatives of all the parishes in the diocese gather and the bishop and priests renew their ordination promises. Most dioceses hold a single celebration of the *Rite of Election* at the cathedral, presided over by the bishop, which is attended by all the adult candidates of the diocese, even though they will be baptised in their local parishes.

In the absence of a priest or deacon, anyone can administer baptism. In countries where there are few priests it is often a lay-catechist who baptises, but in any country if someone is in danger of death and wishes to be baptised, or if a baby is in danger of death and the parents wish him to be baptised, a lay person can and should perform the baptism. There is a special rite for the emergency baptism of an adult, with prayers for the sick person and an opportunity for him to make his profession of faith and promise to undergo proper instruction if he recovers. There is a similar rite for the emergency baptism of a baby, with the parents making the profession of faith; if the baby recovers, there is a special service when he is brought to church and welcomed into the Christian community, during which the parents promise to bring him up in the faith. If, however, there is no time to find the book containing the rite of emergency baptism, all that is necessary is that someone pours water over the candidate, in this manner:

> **John** *(or whatever the name is)*, **I baptise you in the name of the Father,**
> *He pours water over the person.*
> **and of the Son,**
> *He pours water over the person a second time.*
> **and of the Holy Spirit.**
> *He pours water over the person a third time.*

If baptism is given in an emergency by a lay person, he should inform the local Catholic priest as soon as possible, describing what he did, so that the priest can be sure the baptism was carried out properly. The newly baptised person, even if he has only a short time left on earth, is now a member of the Church and part of the parish priest's flock. The local parish will want to be sure he receives all the prayer and support he needs, both before and after his death. When he dies, the parish will pray for him as if he had been a long-time member of the parish community.

The person baptising does not have to be a good Catholic; in fact, he does not even have to be a believer. The minimum that is required is that in good faith he intends to do what the Church intends (even if he is hazy about what this actually is). The reason for this is that it is Christ who is acting, through the baptiser. As St Augustine wrote,

> Peter may baptise, but still it is Christ who baptises; Judas may baptise, but it is still Christ who baptises.

If a person has been baptised in a non-Catholic church and now wishes to become a Catholic, he would not be re-baptised unless there was some doubt about whether the baptism had been carried out properly. In this case he would receive "conditional baptism". Before Vatican II it was common to administer conditional baptism to converts; it has now been recognised, however, that the mainstream Protestant churches all use a baptismal ritual and form of words which fulfils the basic minimum requirement for valid baptism, and therefore conditional baptism is administered rarely. This is not a matter of ecumenical politeness, like supporting each other's church fête. It is part of the Catholic doctrine of the efficacy of sacraments *ex opere operato*. Over a thousand years before the Protestant Reformation the Catholic Church had already faced this question with converts who had been baptised and brought up in the Donatist or Arian churches. Non-Catholic Christians were not re-baptised, because, as one of Augustine's fellow African bishops, Optatus of Milevis, wrote, "All who baptise are labourers not lords, and the sacraments are holy through themselves, not through men."

The Christian community

On the day of the first Christian Pentecost, "Those who received Peter's word were baptised... and they devoted themselves to the apostles' teaching and fellowship" (*Ac* 2:41-42). No one becomes a Christian on his own; no one lives as a Christian on his own - even hermits are linked with the rest of the Church by the bond of prayer and their obedience to the local bishop. Being baptised is not a private matter. It is conceivable that a dying person who wants to be baptised may have no one else there but the priest, but for everyone else the presence of other Christians is immensely important. Those present at a baptism will include some or all of the local Christian community and most importantly the candidate's family and friends, and his sponsors or Godparents.

Family and friends

In the baptism of a baby, there are special prayers for the parents since, as the rite says, they "will be the first teachers of their child in the ways of faith." During the ceremony the parents have a leading role, holding the child during the baptism and making their own promises and profession of faith. At the beginning of the ceremony the priest will say to them:

You are accepting the responsibility of training your child in the practice of the faith. It will be your duty to bring him up to keep God s commandments as Christ taught us, by loving God and our neighbour. Do you clearly understand what you are undertaking?

The Church does not require of the Catholic parents that they should be saints, but they do need to be able to make an honest response to this question.

If one of the parents is not a Catholic, he is still encouraged to take part in so far as his beliefs allow. If there are responses which he feels unable to make, he simply remains silent. Most parishes have a short course of preparation for the parents of babies who are about to be baptised. A non-Catholic parent should be encouraged to attend this course, and to participate in all other aspects of his child's development as a member of the Church. The Catholic parent may be the one who can usually answer the child's questions about the faith, but both parents will help the child to become a mature Christian by their example of honesty and kindness and most of all by giving their child the experience of unconditional love.

Sometimes Catholic parents hesitate to have their child baptised because they themselves feel distant from the Church. This feeling may be the result of some definite estrangement from full participation in the life of the Church, such as being divorced and remarried; it may arise because of a bad experience of the Church in the past, such as encountering a priest or other Catholic who failed to live up to the values of the Gospel; or it could be simply that the Catholic faith has never engaged them in a compelling way. The birth of a baby and the responsibilities this brings are an opportunity to look again at this situation. Those living in a union which has not been blessed by the Church may wish to investigate whether this could be put right. Even if

The faith which they are asked to profess is faith in Jesus Christ, not the attractiveness or perfection of all his followers

this cannot be done, they have still been chosen by God to be the loving parents of this baby whom he loves infinitely and to whom he wishes to give the joy of friendship with Jesus: if they plan to bring up their child in the faith, the Church will welcome the child for baptism. For those who have been put off by unpleasant or simply uninspiring Catholics, their love for their child and their desire to give him the best may be the catalyst for them to explore more deeply what it means to be a disciple of Christ and a member of the Church. The faith which they are asked to profess is faith in Jesus Christ, not the attractiveness or perfection of all his followers. Personal prayer, going to Mass and Confession, friendship with other Catholics, reading the Bible and other books about the faith, and consciously trying to put into practice what one has learned - these are the principal ways in which to develop an adult faith of one's own, and so to be able to be for one's children "the best of teachers", and to make sure that they in turn are not put off Christ or the Church, and even lose their chance of great joy in this world and everlasting happiness in the next.

For adult converts, their non-Catholic relations and friends who wish to come to the baptism should be welcomed with sensitivity and tact. Even if the new Catholic now has beliefs different from theirs, he should make it clear that he still values their love and support and expects to learn from their example of integrity and faithfulness to conscience.

Sponsors or Godparents

In the early Church, when adult baptism was more common, the sponsor or Godparent testified that the candidate showed by his conduct sufficient signs of conversion to Christ to qualify him for baptism. During the fifth century a Spanish nun called Egeria made a pilgrimage to the Holy Land, during which she wrote a lively diary, describing the services for Lent and Easter in Jerusalem, which included the programme for adult catechumens who were to be baptised at the Easter Vigil:

The candidates are led forward, the men with their Godfathers and the women with their Godmothers. Then the bishop questions individually the neighbours of the one who has come up, inquiring: "Does he lead a good life? Does he obey his parents? Is he a drunkard or a liar?"

Godparents have a serious responsibility to assist in their Godchild's development as a Christian

With the predominance of infant baptism the Godparent took the role of making the responses for the infant in the ceremony, and later in contributing to the Christian formation of the child. Today, for adult converts there is no public enquiry about whether the candidate is a drunkard or a liar or anything of that sort. Nevertheless, the Godparent has to testify both at the *Rite of Becoming Catechumens* and the *Rite of Election* that the candidate had accepted Christ as Lord, listens to his word, prays and is worthy to receive baptism. He must promise to help the candidate along his journey through the catechumenate and after baptism as well, by prayer, example and advice.

At the baptism of babies the Godparents are asked if they are ready to help the parents in their duty as Christian mothers and fathers, and they join the parents in making the profession of faith. Godparents have a serious responsibility to assist in their Godchild's development as a Christian. First and foremost, they should pray daily for their Godchild. As the years go by they should look for opportunities to encourage the Christian life of the child, such as buying attractive books about the faith for Christmas and birthdays, attending or at least marking the celebrations for First Holy Communion and Confirmation, arranging outings to places which are both Christian and fun, contributing to anything that enhances the Christian life of the family - even in simple ways like babysitting to give the parents a break - and most of all by being approachable, kind and friendly Catholics. They should be ready to give information and explanations when asked and yet also know how not to be pushy or tactless, remembering that they are merely witnesses to Christ: it is the Holy Spirit who is the advocate, who will do the persuading.

Even for babies, Godparents should be practising Catholics. It may happen that the parents wish to invite two or three friends, including non-Catholics, to act as Godparents. Strictly, the non-Catholic friends cannot be Godparents, but they may be invited to be official witnesses of the baptism; if they subsequently assume a Godparent's role insofar as their beliefs allow, this will no doubt be of benefit to the child and his parents.

7. THE RITE OF BAPTISM IN THE EARLY CHURCH

The baptisms described in the Acts of the Apostles often sound as if they were quite impromptu affairs: Philip the deacon, for example, met an Ethiopian eunuch and at the end of one conversation about the Bible the eunuch said, "See, here is water! What is to prevent my being baptised?" and he was baptised forthwith (*Ac* 8:26-40). Nevertheless, all these accounts of baptisms contain the elements of instruction in the faith, a ritual of baptism and then post-baptismal Christian life. The first Christians were converts from Judaism and therefore already trained in the life of prayer and its expression in everyday conduct. Once non-Jews began to present themselves for baptism, however, it was clear that a long period of preparation was needed, and this is the origin of the Catechumenate process followed by adult converts today.

Did the early Church baptise babies?

When the Acts of the Apostles recounts that a gaoler was baptised "with all his family" (*Ac* 16:33) it is possible that this included children and babies. There is no specific mention of the baptism of babies in the New Testament; on the other hand, there is no mention at all of the baptism of adults who were born and brought up in Christian families, yet one or the other must have happened; perhaps practice varied. The story of Jesus blessing children (*Mk* 10:13-16) may have been recorded to imply that infants could be baptised: the verb "hinder" as in, "Do not hinder them," is in Greek the same as "prevent" in the story of the eunuch. The *Apostolic Tradition* of Hippolytus, written around the turn of the second century, giving instruction about baptism, advises:

> First, baptise the children. Let those who can, speak for themselves. But those unable to speak for themselves, let their parents or someone from the family speak for them. Then, baptise the men, and finally the women.

Origen, writing around 246AD, says that the Church received from the apostles the tradition that even little children should be baptised. His contemporary St Cyprian speaks of baptism on the eighth day after birth as an established custom, but he thought that was too long a delay. Half a century earlier the theologian Tertullian favoured delaying baptism until children were old enough to know Christ, since he did not believe that infants inherited original sin. He also held that baptism should be deferred "for the unmarried, because temptation lies in wait for them, for girls until they reach maturity, and for widows because they have too little to do." This recommendation reveals another theological problem, what could be done about serious sin committed *after* baptism. For many, the solution was to enrol as catechumens but to delay baptism as long as possible: St Augustine, for example, although he had a devout mother in St Monica, was not baptised as a child, a fact he very much regretted. It is partly due to his teaching on original sin that by the sixth century the custom had changed to the baptism of all babies.

How was the actual baptism done?

St Paul's references to baptism as burial with Christ seem to imply that the person disappeared under the water (baptism by submersion). St Cyril of Jerusalem recalls:

> You dipped thrice under the water and thrice rose up again, therein mystically signifying Christ's three days' burial.

On the other hand, the archaeological evidence of early baptismal fonts (rather shallow) and pictorial representations of Christ's baptism in the Jordan would seem to indicate that the candidate stood or knelt in water and either had water poured on him or had just his head dipped under (baptism by immersion). It may have been that practice varied according to local possibilities. The *Didache,* which dates from between the turn of the first century to the middle of the second, briskly advises:

> If you have no running water, baptise in other water;
> and if you cannot in cold, then in warm. But if you
> have neither, pour water on the head three times.

The pouring method is known as "baptism by affusion."
As baptism of infants became the norm, fonts could
become smaller and baptism by affusion was the most
common method. The Church today allows submersion,
or immersion, or affusion.

Anointing

Anointing is not mentioned in the brief accounts of
baptism given by St Justin (martyred 165AD) and in the
Didache. It was however such an intrinsic part of the
bathing customs of the Greco-Roman world, and had
such significance in the religious tradition of Israel, that
it is not unreasonable to speculate that it may have
accompanied Christian baptism from the beginning, and
thus have been the basis for the New Testament
references to Christians as anointed, sealed or made
fragrant. The fuller descriptions of baptism in writings
such as the *Apostolic Tradition* of Hippolytus (martyred
253 AD) or the *Didascalia Apostolorum* (early third
century) discuss pre and post-baptismal anointing in
detail. The Roman Church's custom described by
Hippolytus was for candidates to be anointed by a priest
as soon as they emerged from the water, and then, after

they had dressed, to go before the bishop who laid hands on them, poured chrism on their heads and signed their foreheads with the sign of the cross. Eventually, since increasing numbers meant that the bishop could not be present at all baptisms, this last anointing by the bishop was administered on a later occasion and is the origin of the sacrament of Confirmation we know today.

8. THE RITES OF BAPTISM FOR ADULTS AND BABIES TODAY

As already mentioned, there are different rites for the baptism of adults and infants. They contain the same main elements but in slightly different order, reflecting the fact that for adults there will have been a number of preliminary services already during the catechumenate.

> *becoming a Christian is not a private matter between the Christian and God: it puts us in relationship with the whole Church, on earth and in heaven*

Adults, of course, can make the responses for themselves, and their baptism will take place usually at the Easter Vigil. It is a great joy for a parish community to witness a baptism at the Easter Vigil. A new convert may feel daunted at the prospect of being apparently before everyone's attention on this the greatest night of the Church's year but after all, becoming a Christian is not a private matter between the Christian and God: it puts us in relationship with the whole Church, on earth and in heaven, and even if most of the people present are strangers they are still the Christian family. Converts all confirm that the Easter Vigil is so long and so rich in symbolism that the shyest person is carried along by the grace of the occasion.

At the baptism of babies the parents and godparents make the responses. Babies can be baptised at the Easter Vigil, but the parish Sunday morning Mass may be more practical; the priest and family may even prefer to have the service of baptism separate from Mass, especially if there are other small children in the family who would find Mass too long, or if there are non-Catholic relations who would not feel comfortable at Mass. If there are any difficult family situations which the priest needs to be tactful about, it is wise to warn him privately in good time.

For simplicity, the following account of the baptism of babies is based on this last option, that of a baptismal service separate from Mass.

If the baptism of babies takes place during Mass, the *opening rite* of the baptism happens at the beginning of Mass, the actual *baptism* part (the Celebration of the Sacrament) happens after the sermon, and the *concluding rites* of the baptism take place at the end of Mass, after Holy Communion.

If babies or adults are to be baptised at the Easter Vigil, the opening rite of the baptism and the baptism itself take place after the sermon, and the concluding rites of the baptism take place at the end of Mass, after Holy Communion.

Reception of the child

Welcome

Naming of the child

The priest asks the parents what name they have chosen. A baptismal name must be the name of a saint or have Christian significance. If the baby is to have a name of no Christian significance, another Christian name should be added. The great figures of the Old Testament are counted as saints, so their names can be used: for example, the Archbishop of Paris, Cardinal Lustiger, came from a non-believing Jewish family and was baptised as a teenager; he kept his Jewish name Aron (Aaron) but added Jean-Marie. For adult converts there is a special service on Holy Saturday morning, before the baptism at the Easter Vigil, when they state what baptismal names they have chosen.

The parents promise to bring up the child in the faith and the Godparents promise to help.

For adult converts, there is a service during Lent in which the Creed is formally presented to them; they learn it by heart and recite it publicly at the service on Holy Saturday morning. Since the baby cannot do this, the parents and Godparents are committing themselves to providing the environment and teaching which should enable him to do so one day.

The priest makes the sign of the cross
on the baby's forehead;
parents and godparents do the same if they wish.

For adult converts, it is at the start of the catechumenate programme that the candidate is welcomed at the entrance of the church and signed with the sign of the cross. Regarding the sign of the cross, St Cyril of Jerusalem told the newly baptised, "Here is a great protection that is free for the poor and easy for the weak, since grace comes from God. It is a sign for the faithful and a terror for demons."[3] The parents may wish to bless their child daily in this way, until he can make the sign of the cross himself and begin to know the Person who died on the cross for him.

All enter church in procession while a suitable hymn is sung

Celebration of God's word

Readings from Scripture; sermon

There is a huge choice of readings. The parish priest will have the full list in a book, and parents and Godparents would find it enriching to look at them all.

---

[3] St Cyril of Jerusalem, *Mystagogical Catecheses* 13.36. The great writers of the early Church loved discoursing on the symbolism of the various aspects of the baptismal rite, and only brief references can be given here. The reader is referred to the list of books for further reading, given at the end of this booklet.

Intercessory prayers

There are several forms of these prayers and if the family have special intentions extra prayers may be added: they should discuss this beforehand with the priest.

Short litany of saints

For adults there is the full litany of saints. For both adults and babies the patron saints of the new Christian are included, and any others of special significance such as the patron saints of the church or of members of the family

Prayer of exorcism

For adult converts there are prayers of exorcism at each of the Scrutinies (the special services on the Sundays in Lent). For both adults and babies the prayers of exorcism are short and undramatic, simply recognising that the world which God loves is flawed by evil and the snares of the devil, but that the Son of God has come to rescue man from this evil and bring him into the splendour of God's kingdom of light.

Anointing with oil of catechumens (plain oil)

An adult receives this anointing on Holy Saturday morning. The oil of catechumens signifies readiness for the battle with sin and evil, of which baptism is the opening salvo.

Celebration of the Sacrament

Blessing of water

There are several forms of this blessing which can be chosen. The first recalls the great acts of salvation which have involved water (creation, Noah's flood, the crossing of the Red Sea) and especially the water and blood which flowed from the side of Jesus as he hung on the cross. The other forms of the blessing stress the new life which baptism brings. The first form of the blessing of water ends with the congregation responding "Amen"; the others expect the response "Blessed be God" at several stages: the parents and priest may be influenced in their choice by their knowledge of what the family and friends will be comfortable saying.

If the baptism is taking place at the Easter Vigil, the priest plunges the paschal candle into the water in the baptismal font. Some politely interpret this ancient gesture as a symbol of death and resurrection but the accompanying prayer for new life, and the womb-shape of the font, suggest that our ancestors had a more vigorous imagination. The mutual love of the parents brought this baby into existence on earth; the love of Christ, dwelling within the Christian community, now offers him life which will last for ever.

Renunciation of the devil and sin; Profession of faith (by parents and godparents)

There is no suggestion that the baby or even the adult candidate is possessed by Satan as in modern horror

films. When an adult makes this renunciation of Satan
and profession of faith in Jesus Christ he is making a
definitive statement of his allegiance, a public
proclamation of what set of values he wants to govern
his life. Since a baby cannot do this, the parents and
Godparents make this statement about whom they see as
the ultimate Lord of the world, and by whose values they
plan to bring up this child.

Baptism

As already explained, the baptism can be done by pouring
water over or fully immersing the candidate. What usually
happens is that the mother holds the baby over the font and
the priest pours water over the baby's head, while saying
"John [or whatever the name is], I baptise you in the name
of the Father and of the Son and of the Holy Spirit."

Anointing with chrism

After baptism the baby is anointed with perfumed oil called
chrism. This is a sign of honour, marking out the newly
baptised baby as a member of the body of Christ who was
anointed as priest, prophet and king. A newly baptised
adult usually receives the sacrament of confirmation at the
same Mass and so does not receive this anointing.

Clothing in a white garment

Theodore of Mopsuestia calls the white garment
(nowadays usually a white shawl) "a sign to the world of

shining splendour and the way of life to which you have already passed in symbol" while St John Chrysostom urged his converts, "Let us be eager to preserve this beauty in its full bloom and let us learn what can keep it bright."

Presentation of a lighted candle
Someone from the baby's family lights a candle from the paschal candle and holds it on behalf of the baby. For an adult convert the candle is formally presented to him with the words: "You have been enlightened by Christ. Walk always as children of the light;" but in the case of a baby the parents are told, "This light is entrusted to you to be kept burning brightly." In some parishes at this stage lighted candles are handed to everyone in the family capable of holding one. A non-Catholic who loves the child and plans to do his best for him, even if not sharing his religious faith, can appropriately hold a candle as a symbol of this, if he wishes. St Gregory Nazianzen told the newly baptised at Constantinople, "The lamps which you will light symbolise the torchlight procession in the next world, in which our shining, virgin souls will meet the bridegroom with the shining lights of faith."

Rite of Ephphetha
Ephphetha is the Aramaic word Jesus used when he cured a deaf and dumb man (*Mk* 7:31-37). For an adult this little ceremony takes place on Holy Saturday morning: the priest touches the candidate's ears and

mouth and prays that he may profess the faith he has heard. For a newly baptised baby the prayer looks forward to the child's future profession of faith: "May he soon touch your ears to receive his word, and your mouth to proclaim his faith."

Conclusion of the rite

Our Father
For adults, the initiation into the Church is completed by the sacraments of Confirmation and Holy Communion. For babies, the priest and congregation look forward to these developments by saying, in the child's name, the Our Father.

Special blessing of the mother, then the father,
then the child, and finally the whole congregation.
There are several forms of this blessing which can be chosen: the answer to each part is "Amen."

9. My Soul Magnifies the Lord

Reflecting on the first days after his baptism at the age of twenty-three, Thomas Merton wrote:

One of the big defects of my spiritual life in that first year was a lack of devotion to the Mother of God... I said the "Hail Mary" when I prayed, but that is not enough... I did not have that sense of dependence or of her power I had to find out by experience.

The *Rite of Baptism for Children,* when not celebrated during Mass, should conclude with a hymn of Easter joy, or with the Magnificat, the Canticle of Mary (*Lk* 1:46-55). Some families even place the baby on the altar before Mary's statue, invoking her maternal care and intercession for the new little Christian. This involvement of Mary, while not formally part of the rite, is not just a pious frill but rather the ordinary Christian doing instinctively what has been theorised about by the theologians. Honour paid to Mary, and the Catholic beliefs about the sacraments, are both spin-offs, logical developments, of the doctrine of the Incarnation, God becoming man, taking flesh in Mary's womb, so that he who created the universe and continues to hold it in being was nourished by Mary's body and brought up by her. The flesh-and-blood Jesus who could be touched lovingly by Mary and the disciples, and roughly by his enemies, and even spat upon, flogged and crucified, is no longer ours to see or touch. We believe that, through the resurrection, the flesh-and-blood body of Jesus has not decayed into dust but is transformed in glory. The barriers between the glory of heaven and the manifest non-glory of this world of sin and death have been broken down. A Catholic will turn as naturally to Mary to ask her prayers as he will to the friend in the next pew. The Church takes ordinary things - water, oil, bread, wine, even the act of love between husband and wife - and finds in them the vehicles of God's life and a foretaste of the life of heaven. However sinful the candidate for baptism, or however small and helpless, he can sing with Mary, "He has looked on his servant in her lowliness... The Almighty has done great things for me." The realm of evil may seem to hold sway but "He has put forth his arm in strength and scattered the proud-hearted; he has put down the mighty from their seat." The new life given in baptism is the beginning of the fulfilment of all the Old Testament promises "to Abraham and his sons" and the desires of every human heart.

Baptism is God's most beautiful and magnificent gift.
We call it gift, grace, anointing,
enlightenment, garment of immortality, bath of rebirth,
seal and most precious gift.

It is called *gift* because it is conferred on those who bring nothing of their own;

grace since it is given even to the guilty;

baptism because sin is buried in the water;

anointing for it is priestly and royal as are those who are anointed;

enlightenment because it radiates light;

clothing since it veils our shame;

bath because it washes;

and *seal* as it is our guard and the sign of God's Lordship.

(St Gregory Nazianzen, homily on baptism,
preached on 6 January 381AD)

FURTHER READING

Since this booklet may be read by the non-Catholic parent of a Catholic baby, or the non-Catholic spouse or friend of an adult convert, a few general introductions to Christianity have been included.

Booklets:

On the Sacraments:

Baptism (CTS Publications, 2004; Do 712).
Confirmation (CTS Publications, 2004; Do 713).
Eucharist (CTS Publications, 2004; Do 714).
Reconciliation (CTS Publications, 2004; Do 716).
Anointing (CTS Publications, 2004; Do 711).
Marriage (CTS Publications, 2004; Do 710).
Holy Orders (CTS Publications, 2004; Do 715).

On Christianity in general:

A Catechism of Christian Doctrine (CTS Publications, 1997; Do 003).

Jones, David Albert OP, *Christianity: an introduction to the Catholic faith* (Family Publications, Oxford, 1999).

Jones, David Albert OP, *Why be a Catholic?* (CTS Publications, 1996; Do 642); this booklet was based on talks given to a mixed group of Catholics and Evangelical Protestants, so may be useful to someone with a Protestant background.

McCabe, Herbert OP, *The teaching of the Catholic Church: a new catechism of Christian Doctrine* (Darton, Longman & Todd, 2000).

Heftier tomes

On baptism and the Sacraments

Baker, J Robert, Nyberg, Larry J, Tufano, Victoria M, *A Baptism Sourcebook* (Chicago, Liturgy Training Publications, 1993): this is an anthology of texts, ancient and modern, about baptism.

Finn, Thomas M, *Early Christian Baptism and the Catechumenate: Italy, North Africa and Egypt* (Liturgical Press, 1992).

Finn, Thomas M, *Early Christian Baptism and the Catechumenate: West and East Syria* (Liturgical Press, 1992).

Kavanagh, Aidan OSB, *The Shape of Baptism: the rite of Christian initiation* (Pueblo, 1978).

Schillebeeckx, Edward, *Christ the Sacrament* (Sheed & Ward, 1963).

Searle, Mark, *Christening: the making of Christians* (Kevin Mayhew, 1980).

Yarnold, Edward SJ, *The awe-inspiring rites of initiation: baptismal homilies of the fourth century* (St Paul Publications, 1971).

On Christianity in general:

Catechism of the Catholic Church (Geoffrey Chapman, 1994).

Nichols, Aidan OP, *Epiphany: a theological introduction to Catholicism* (Liturgical Press, 1996); contains comprehensive suggestions for further reading.

Strange, Roderick: *The Catholic Faith* (Hodder & Stoughton, 2001).

Informative Catholic Reading

We hope that you have enjoyed reading this booklet.

If you would like to find out more about CTS booklets - we'll send you our free information pack and catalogue.

Please send us your details:

Name ....

Address ....

....

....

Postcode ....

Telephone...

Email ....

Send to: CTS, 40-46 Harleyford Road,
           Vauxhall, London
           SE11 5AY

Tel: 020 7640 0042
Fax: 020 7640 0046
Email: info@cts-online.org.uk

 **CTS**